LIGHTNING BOLT BOOKS™

The Wildebeest's Journey

Jon M. Fishman

Lerner Publications • Minneapolis

Lerner Publications Company
A division of Lerner Publishing Group, Inc.
241 First Avenue North
Minneapolis, MN 55401 USA

For reading levels and more information, look up this title at www.lernerbooks.com.

The Cataloging-in-Publication Data for *The Wildebeest's Journey* is on file at the Library of Congress.
ISBN 978-1-5124-8638-4 (lib. bdg.)
ISBN 978-1-5415-1185-9 (pbk.)
ISBN 978-1-5124-9814-1 (eb pdf)

Manufactured in the United States of America
1-43462-33202-6/9/2017

Table of Contents

Meet the Wildebeest

A wildebeest walks through an African grassland. Wildebeests are migrators. They move from one area to another at different times of the year.

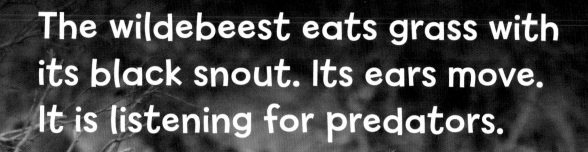

The wildebeest eats grass with its black snout. Its ears move. It is listening for predators.

A wildebeest's long ears help it hear predators.

Wildebeests have two curved horns on top of their heads. A black mane goes down their necks to the middle of their backs. They have a beard below their heads that is black or white.

Wildebeests use their long tails to swat away flies.

Wildebeests live in southern and eastern Africa.

Wildebeests live in large groups called herds. Herds go on long journeys to find fresh water and grass.

A Wildebeest Is Born

A female wildebeest walks with her herd. Then she lies down on her side. She is giving birth to a baby. The baby wildebeest is called a calf.

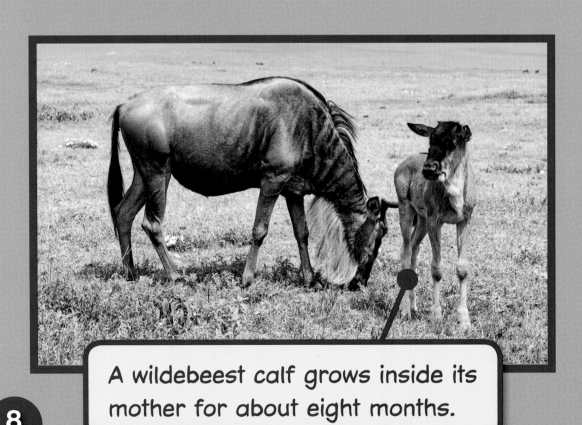

A wildebeest calf grows inside its mother for about eight months.

A mother wildebeest protects her calf from predators.

Wildebeest mothers give birth to a single calf once a year. The calf can stand on its own within fifteen minutes of birth. It needs to be able to move quickly with the herd.

A calf drinks its mother's milk for its first six to nine months. It begins eating grass ten days after it is born.

An adult wildebeest weighs up to 600 pounds (272 kg). That's about the weight of an adult pig.

Male wildebeests leave their mother's herd after one year. They join groups of other male wildebeests. Someday they will form their own migrating herds.

A Wildebeest Migrates

A wildebeest herd stretches across a grassland. It is April, and the herd is migrating north. They follow the rain. Different parts of Africa get more rain as the seasons change.

The wildebeest herd splashes through a river. *Chomp!* A crocodile grabs a wildebeest and drags it underwater. Many wildebeests are eaten by predators along the way.

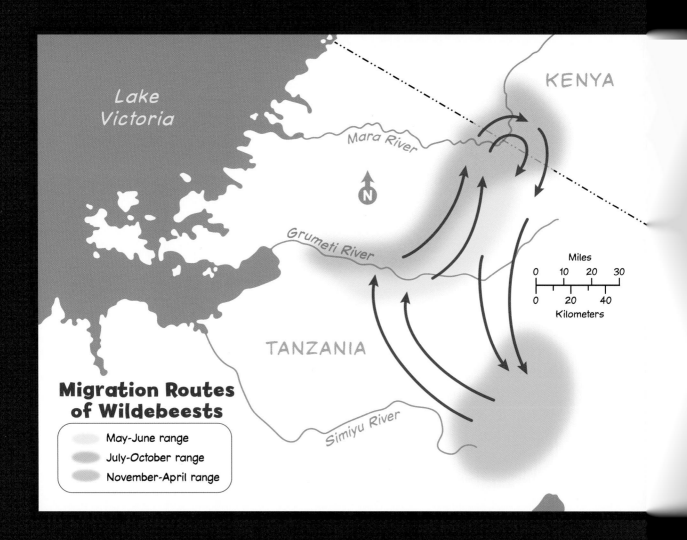

Lake Victoria

KENYA

Mara River

N

Grumeti River

Miles
0   10   20   30

0   20   40
Kilometers

TANZANIA

Migration Routes of Wildebeests

- May–June range
- July–October range
- November–April range

Simiyu River

The herd travels for more than four months. Finally, the herd reaches the place where it will spend the fall season in southwestern Kenya.

In November, the wildebeest herds migrate south again. They will have more calves. By April, the wildebeests will be ready for their next journey north.

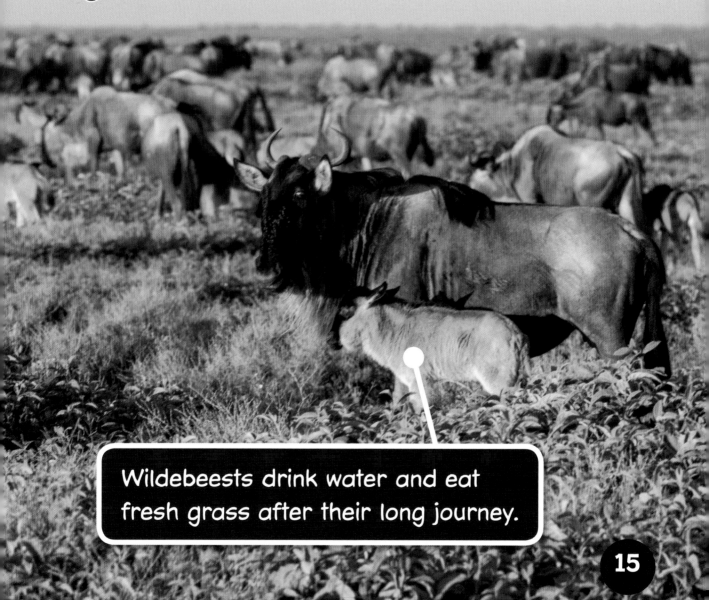

Wildebeests drink water and eat fresh grass after their long journey.

Wildebeests in Danger

Earth's climate is changing. In some places, less rain falls than in the past. During a drought, wildebeests suffer.

Bang! A gunshot echoes through the air. Hunting is another danger for wildebeests. People hunt wildebeests for their meat.

The flat grasslands where wildebeests spend much of their time make them easy for hunters to spot.

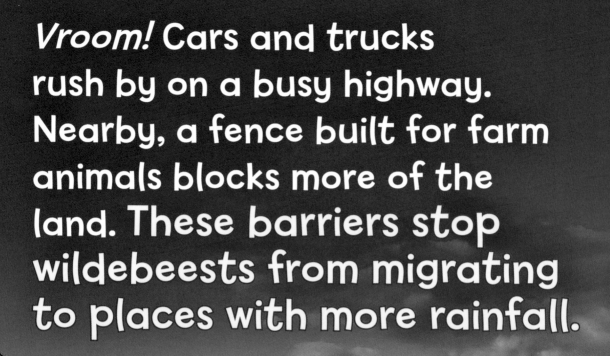

Vroom! Cars and trucks rush by on a busy highway. Nearby, a fence built for farm animals blocks more of the land. These barriers stop wildebeests from migrating to places with more rainfall.

Wildebeests can't migrate when they are blocked by roads and fences.

People cause a lot of harm to wildebeests. But some people are working to keep wildebeests' migration paths clear of fences and roads. They want to make sure the wildebeest herds can keep making their long journey to follow the rain.

Fun Facts

- *Wildebeest* means "wild beast" in a language called Afrikaans. Wildebeests are also called gnus, which you say like "news."

- Up to five hundred thousand baby wildebeests are born at the beginning of the spring rainy season. The calves each weigh about 45 pounds (20 kg) at birth.

- Climate change and human activity have reduced the number of wildebeests in Africa. But there are still enough to form huge herds. More than 1.5 million wildebeests migrate each year.

More Amazing Migrators

- Caribou are large deer that spend summer on the northern coast of Alaska. As winter nears, herds of caribou migrate southeast to spend the season in warmer parts of Canada.

- Huge groups of bison used to migrate in the United States. Herds with as many as four million animals followed the rainy weather. The size of bison herds is smaller due to human activity.

- The zebra is another large African animal that migrates. Thousands of zebras travel hundreds of miles each year.

Glossary

climate: the average weather in an area over a period of years

drought: a long period with little rain

grassland: a large area that is covered in grasses and has few trees

mane: long hair on an animal's neck

migrator: an animal that moves from one area to another at different times of the year

predator: an animal that eats other animals

snout: the mouth and nose of an animal

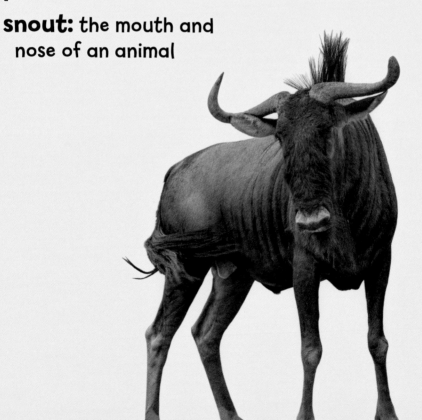

Further Reading

Africa Facts
http://www.kids-world-travel-guide.com
/africa-facts.html

Bowman, Chris. *Wildebeests*. Minneapolis: Bellwether Media, 2015.

Ducksters: Animal Migrations
http://www.ducksters.com/animals/animal
_migrations.php

Kopp, Megan. *Migration*. New York: Smartbook Media Inc., 2017.

Owings, Lisa. *Meet a Baby Zebra*. Minneapolis: Lerner Publications, 2016.

Index

Photo Acknowledgments

The images in this book are used with the permission of: Stephanie Periquet/Shutterstock.com, pp. 2, 6; iStockphoto.com/Byrdyak , p. 4; iStockphoto.com/VHcreations, p. 5; iStockphoto.com/yenwen, p. 7; imageBROKER/Alamy Stock Photo, p. 8; Wandel Guides/Shutterstock.com, p. 9; Ariadne Van Zandbergen/Alamy Stock Photo, p. 10; GUDKOV ANDREY/Shutterstock.com, p. 11; iStockphoto.com/1001slide, pp. 12, 13; © Laura Westlund/Independent Picture Service, p. 14; Laura Romin & Larry Dalton/Alamy Stock Photo, p.15; iStockphoto.com/AOosthuizen, p. 16; © Oleg Znamenskiy/Bigstock.com, p. 17; Francois Loubser/Shutterstock.com, p. 18; Gail Johnson/Shutterstock.com, p. 19; WOLF AVNI/Shutterstock.com, p. 22.

Front cover: Pearl Media/Shutterstock.com

Main body text set in Billy Infant regular 28/36. Typeface provided by SparkType.